WHERE THE BIRDS SING BASS

WHERE THE BIRDS SING BASS

Reginald Lockett

Jukebox Press

Oakland, California

No part of this book may be reproduced in any form by any means, electronic or mechanical, including photocopying, recording, or information retrieval system, without written permission from the publisher.

Grateful acknowledgement is hereby made to the following anthologies and periodicals in which some of these poems and the memoir have appeared:

Maybe Mombassa, Yellow Silk, Blue Unicorn, Black Scholar, Appeal to Reason, Star-Web Paper, Erotique Noir/Black Erotica, Quilt, BOP, Iowa Review, BlackWorld, 14 Voices, Visions Across the Americas, California Childhood, Because You Talk and *Loose Leaf*.

Cover Photo: Lewis Watts
Cover Design: Billy Richardson and Reginald Lockett
Author Photo: Kathy Sloane

Library of Congress Catalogue Number 88-093046
ISBN 0-932693-05-9

Copyright© by Reginald Lockett
All rights reserved.

*This book is dedicated to
my daughters
Maya Lomasi and Lauren Aimee*

Contents

Back In The Day

Oaktown, CA	3
3 Tales From Growin Up In The 60's	5
By Way Of A Eulogy	8
Triple Feature	10
Groovin & Boppin At The Eastern City Cafe	12

Real Folks and Heroes

Endless Ports Of Call	16
Driving Maya Home	19
MOM	21
They Like To See Me Eat	24
August, 1958	27
They Want Me To Get A Steady Job	30
Aunt Lola's Take On Black History	32
For My Cousin, De Mayor	34
Sunday Morning	35
An Urgent Visual Message from the Poet	38

How I Started Writing Poetry   40

What It Be Like

What You See Ain't What You Are	51
The Silent Songwriter Of Our Apocalypse	53
Song Of Fire	55
Ramses' Dance	57
A Lesson In Aesthetics	59

Bro. Radio & Me

Bro. Radio & Me	63
Bro. Radio's New Occupation	65
Radio In Love	66
Bro. Radio's Paranoia	67
Bro. Radio & My Kind Of Women	68
Bro. Radio's Protest	69

Gettin Some. . .

A Kite Poem For You	73
Untitled	74
The X-Lovers	75
405 Scott Street	77
Cheeseburgers	79
Shoulda-Coulda-Woulda	80

Funky Truths and Realities

Good Times & No Bread	85
The Movement	87
When They Came To Take Him	90
Prediction	92
She Tries: Reflections On A Student's Homework Assignment	93
The Terminator	95
Pamela: A Case of Extreme Abuse	97
A Child Of Our Revolution	99
Occupational Lycanthropy	101
Superstition	104
Are We What We Eat?	106
Meditation On A Get-Together For Ted At Jim's House	108

Back In The Day

Oaktown, CA

Absorbing a taste of magic,
trying to figure the flavor,
twelve minutes past midnight,
Thursday morning,
walking somewhere on San Pablo.
I stop in an obscure juke joint
for two, three beers.
Tinkling sound of a quarter
in the jukebox.
Blues twanging guitar.
Lucille putting it
down on the table where
you can see it, feel it,
and know it's real.
Man rocking to her
electric,
sensuous rhythms.
Eyes shut tight.
White and gold teeth flashing
on his paint smeared
black face.
Lucille, B.B.'s lady,
talking about "Friends".
Friends.
I remember them
in the right light
in Friday and Saturday
evening breezes,
harmonizing, signifying, and

guzzling Greystone, Thunderbird,
Ripple and Green Death.
I think about the way
the purple, yellow, red, pink,
and loud sky baby blue slacks, sweaters,
and coats
that beamed in the street light's glow.
The Stacey Adams and alligator shoes
that smiled.
Sweet Charlie,
fried, dyed,
and laid to the side
in a one button Continental suit,
High Boy shirt, wide paisley tie and burgundy
pimp shades, winning every game
at Moon's Pool Hall.
Cadillac dreamers hanging in there
where we still die unnatural deaths
at the hands of imported cracker cops,
anal retentive educators,
mentally constipated politicians,
and conceptually incarcerated
drug dealers
in a town, in a town, in a town,
in a state, in a state, in a state,
in a nation, in a nation, in a nation
so bad,
even the birds sing bass.

3 Tales From Growin Up In The 60's

#1

Billy Boo used to pile on six t-shirts,
two pullover sweaters, and a thick
Pendleton shirt. All tucked neatly
in his khakis or black Ben Davidsons
for that buffed, muscle-bound look.
Any kind of weather. Didn't matter
to him if it was 94 in the shade
in the middle of July. The style
of his marcelled hair reminded me
of a steep cliff in one of them
old cowboy flicks. Sort of looked
like the one in the Prudential Insurance
commercials. Just like "a piece of the rock."
Must've been the way the pompadour
swooped out into a ledge and then
shot straight down to the hairline
on his forehead. Standin out in front
of the liquor store on 36th and San Pablo
sippin white port and lemon juice. Cool.
Goin for bad until some real hoodlum
from Campbell Village (or was it Harbor Homes?)
with the real biceps, the sho nuff triceps,
the Arm & Hammer Baking Soda forearms,
and sledgehammer fists, beat the Pendleton,
both sweaters, all six t-shirts, and the khakis
right off of Billy Boo's weak, boney body.

#2

It was around this time,
doin detention, after school,
in Miss Belasco's art class
for talkin about the bags under
her eyes that skinny Harold Kendricks
took it upon himself to hip me
to everything he thought I
needed to know about sex. Would draw
pictures of tits and vaginas while tellin
me how to rap, kiss, what to feel on,
and how to jump off
in some twanks and stroke. Told me the pimples
on my face were pussy bumps, and
that I'd better start gettin some trim
or end up just like
Crater Face Jerome with the big,
quarter size pus bumps
all over his face.

#3

At home alone, Bean Juice
took a notion to give himself
one of them do-it-yourself
conks. Read the directions
carefully and, as instructed, massaged
the Dixie Peach into his scalp. Then
he put in the strong, lye based
King Konk. Combed it in real good

and let it set until it started
burnin. Got up to
rinse it out in the kitchen sink.
No water! Last month's bill hadn't been paid.
Head sizzlin, he made a dash for
the bathroom. Face bowl. Nothin. Tub. Unh-unh.
Toilet. Unflushed. Head feelin
white hot—like it could melt
—Bean Juice ran the whole six blocks to
the fire station on 34th and Market
where, instead of a water hose,
they used a fire extinguisher.

By Way Of A Eulogy

in memory of Leroy Payne

Out for a good time. That's
the way I want to remember him.
Always out for a real get-on-down
good time. Hair half-gassed back
red. The weekend-go-party
mint green suit and knob toed,
rust colored Staceys to match. Digging
Jackie Wilson and James Brown
drive the ladies wild. Trying
to cop their styles.
Never without that ever present 35 cent
shortneck of Greystone or Thunderbird
tightly wrapped in a twisted,
crumpled paper bag. Him and his buddies.
They were always four, five, six years
older. Eighteen, nineteen,
twenty. I was thirteen
going on fourteen. Pompadoured marcels
and processes blowing in the wind,
these workers at Del Monte,
uninvited party guests,
would let me low ride with them
up, down, and around North and West Oakland
in muscle-bound King's yellow '57
Buick Roadmaster with the big, thick
white walls. Leroy
used to piss me off when he'd buy wine

for all the fellas—and a root beer
for me. He kept
forgetting I wasn't a kid no more.
Anyhow,
the girls didn't like you
if you didn't act like no man, and
drinking wine and smoking cigarettes
were the best ways to prove it
outside of getting your ass kicked
trying to thump on some dude
you didn't know doodley-squat about.
That's how long I been knowing
Leroy. Some time later, when he was
twenty-five, pushing a hard twenty-six,
he got drafted. Eleven months in Nam.
Back to Oakland, family, friends,
the cannery, the wine and good times.
That's how I like to remember Leroy.
About a week and a half ago,
Leroy came in from a night of partying nonstop
with three shortnecks
of Greystone and a few Schlitz Bulls
in tow. Laid down to rest,
and never got to bust the caps
on them cans. You see, Leroy crashed
a party in Paradise,
and refused to leave.

Triple Feature

for Robert Hayden

The Roxie, Lux, Broadway, Globe,
and, yes, the T&D are all gone now.
Old movie theaters that had
lost all their grandeur long
before we, the children of the newly arrived
from all points South,
converged on them every Saturday
for three horror filled spectaculars,
two cartoons, previews,
stale popcorn, soda gone flat,
roaches crawling on the screen,
and, always, the rats
casually sauntering across stage.

Totally unenthralled with "The Giant Behemoth",
"Teenaged Werewolf", "Hideous Sun Demon",
or overgrown grasshoppers in "The Beginning of the End",
we were the real creatures
who starred in those triple features
with our ice and food fights, roving hands, spitballs,
and neighborhood gang disputes.

And as we went about our monstrous tasks—
stealing the snackbar blind, kicking over trashcans,
smashing restroom mirrors,
and peeing all over some chump usher's uniform

—a bewildered, jittery middle-aged manager
would threaten to call the law,
throw us all out, and close the place down,
only to end up like the mad scientist
in one of the monster flicks,
attacked by his own creations
gone awry.

Groovin & Boppin At The Eastern City Cafe

for Ishmael Reed & Bob Callahan

Tacked to the wall,
paper plates
signed by blues legends,
baseball players & football stars
reminisce
right next to the menu
written out in chalk
on a blackboard
advertisin liver
smothered in onions, ox tails
over rice, neck bones,
collard greens & blackeye peas
side by side with
the sweet & sour pork,
chicken fried rice
& egg foo yung.
Me & good runnin buddy Ron
snap our fingers to the rhythm
of the Pointer Sisters' excitement
& croon "Joanna" in sync
with Kool & The Gang
in this San Pablo Ave. restaurant
catercornered
somewhere between
the Oakland & Emeryville city limits.
Somethin else totally alien
to boundaries known & seen.

The legacies & recollections
lurkin in the booths or sittin
bent forward at the counter
has kept them comin in droves
generation after generation
to this place
on the edge of the boonies
where caramel brown
& creamy chocolate waitresses,
fine, foxy, sweet women
of this city's past,
get older with each order taken
as the cooks yammer away in Cantonese
back in the kitchen where the Congo,
the Mississippi, and the Yangtze
merge in a torrent
of continuous rapport.

Real Folks and Heroes

Endless Ports Of Call

for my father, Jewell Lockett, SDCM, USN (Ret.)

With retirement back there
almost twenty years ago (and that gig
with the school district, fourteen of them),
he's still very Navy. My father,
who at twenty-three walked away
from the straight and narrow poverty
surrounding his father's East Texas farm
to the straight and narrow routines of galleys
and officers' mess halls on cruisers, destroyers,
supply ships and carriers through three wars.
Even after snapping to attention and saluting
for the last time aboard the man o' war Ranger,
it continues to be the scrutiny of some authority
hovering there, in the back of his mind,
that keeps the hedges trimmed, the lawn well
manicured,
the steps and sidewalk swept, the rows of
vegetables
in meticulous, arrow straight lines,
and the house never in need of paint. Is it
being forever ready for a sneak inspection
that keeps every pair of shoes he owns
spit shined and the blues, grays, tans, blacks, and
whites
he strolls so erect in on Sundays cleaned and
neatly pressed?
Yes, it's still "swab the deck" instead of "mop

the floor,"
"secure the door" as opposed to simply locking it,
and "break out the chow" when "serve the table"
will do. And what
of those years of me fronting, wanting to be one
with those
who talked that talk and walked that walk,
doing a continuous dress rehearsal of fantasies
that were popsicles melting and evaporating
under the heat of hot, blazing realities? How many
times
did he suddenly, unexpectedly appear
in geometry, history, or English Comp.
in full Navy dress blues with the gold chevron
of a master chief steward and five hash marks
on the left sleeve a show of authority
and years of service, and that grin
just like the one Scatman Crothers wore,
the whole ghetto classroom in awe of him? I,
a budding Slick Draw McGraw, would slide halfway
down in my seat in part shy, timid pride,
part adolescent disgust because my facade
of daring-do, cool con man bravado
had been blown in full view of my homeboys. This
man,
this sailor, my father would sit quietly
and attentively two, three seats behind me,
pushing me, urging me
beyond the loneliness of tight, steamy kitchens,
above the lunacy
of another man's glory, onward to other shores of

the senses,
where the boats of true warriors set sail
to endless ports of call.

Driving Maya Home

Dainty little hands
still clutching toothpaste
and brush
she's just rediscovered
for the umpteeth time
in a week, and hanging
onto that green Care Bear
for dear life, she nods,
bending forward,
close to the window,
in a relentless battle
with the Sandman
she'll never win.
My daughter, cuddled
by the slow, mellow music
Daddy loves
and cooled by the warm
night air,
soars higher and farther
out there in that world
created for her dreams only.
Riding shotgun
for me, the original Rhythm & Blues poet,
harmonizing to a tune on the radio,
her soft, easy breaths
fog the passenger door window,
blotting out all this angry,
frustrated hopelessness
that sprouts

from the sidewalks and flourishes
in the projects we pass
going home down E. 14th.

MOM

the cartilage
barely   attached
to the bones
in both knees. her
right arm is weak
                and
gives out   at
the elbow. way overweight,
she's been classified
handicapped,   and can't
                get out much
like she
used to. cooking, washing,
cleaning,
or anything pertaining
             to work
are misplaced words
in her vocabulary.   food
comes her way
                from relatives
and that new county
program
         for the disabled.
then there's Concepcion
                who comes in
to clean,   console
                and chastise
once every week. though

she shouldn't have it,
                      five piece orders
of Golden Bird
            fried chicken,
barbequed beef,
                smothered
in sweet sauce,
                from Gadbury's
      and
Bicardi light with coke
somehow appears
                through
the good graces of a niece,
nephew, cousin,
                or a friend. right there
in the back house
on E. Gage Avenue in the City of Angels,
she keeps close tabs
        on
her favorite daytime and evening
                soaps
among old and new photos
                of
three sons grown and gone,
and a grandson and granddaughter
born
      too late in her life
                    to
toddle behind her
            in the yard
or tag along to a neighborhood store

anticipating
        the multi-colored popsicle
or chocolate and nut covered ice cream
                            bar
rewarded for toting
        a sparsely
filled bag of fruit, vegetables or meat.
fiercely defiant
        in her stubborn convictions,
she sometimes   speaks
        of
that head-on, inevitable
        meeting
with death and how she'd
        like things
arranged. when
we three sons moan, "ahh mom!"
                in
still perfect harmony, she
        chuckles,
cocks her head
        to that favored
right angled slant
        and
just looks far off
        into a distance
we three have yet not begun
to travel.

They Like To See Me Eat

for Joyce Carol Thomas & Angela Jackson

they never come
right out and say they think i'm too
thin to their liking.
these two women in my life.
no.
they just insinuate it with
a passing mention of the
boyish looks gone, the
sinking of the cheeks, deepening
of the eyes
and sagginess in the
seat of the pants,
these big-boned women from
the pine forests of East Texas
whose wills were cast
in Benin bronze.
home remedied, liniment saturated
tallow rags and ace bandages
wrapped around stiff-jointed necks,
knees, and ankles, they move
about the roomy kitchen
praising the tenderness of the mustards,
freshness of the snap beans,
fluffy lightness of the cornbread,
and golden crispyness of the
chicken or fish fried.

these women
look on in despair and disgust
when i reach for a tiny saucer
to nibble a dab of this, a skoasha of that
and a paltry wing instead of
the humungous breast i loved as a child
growing up in this house.
my mother and aunt then allude
to that new lemon yogurt pie
recipe they've just tried out
that's made with lemon flavored yogurt,
Eagle Brand Condensed Milk,
and whipping cream,
all in a ready-to-serve graham cracker crust,
since i'm now into health foods,
watching my weight and all that.
then they talk about
an article they read
in a magazine or newspaper somewhere
where the doctors are saying
all this jogging, exercising, and
eating natural foods ain't good for you;
and that a little extra weight
ain't never hurt nobody.
these two women love to see me eat.
worries don't follow them to bed
because, with the opening and closing
of the oven and slamming of the refrigerator door,

they know
the icebox commando
rides at midnight

August, 1958

with the sound

of a familiar car

turning swiftly

off the road,

chickens

cackling and scattering,

and the dog barking,

she stuck

her Choctaw tinged

afroid face

outside

the door.

after

welcoming me,

her grandchild,

with hugs, kisses,

chuckles,

and a tear or two,

she then

went about the business

of righting

my spoiled, wild,

wayward city ways

with GOD

entrenched in her soul,

LOVE

deep in her heart,

SURVIVAL

heavy on her mind

and a bundle

of freshly cut

green switches

in the freezer.

they want me to get a steady job

they want me to hold down a steady job,
get good medical and dental coverage,
a fourth life insurance policy, membership
in the company's credit union and accrue sick,
annual and vacation time. if they could have
their way,
my parents would have me become
the perfect example
of straight, clean, secure living.
I'd be on the steward board or in the choir
of some large United Methodist church
and contribute a juicy chunk of my
salary every month. also
be well known in the community. I'd have
an angel of a wife who wouldn't
drink, smoke, cuss,
wear rings in her nose, flaming red
lipstick, braids or cornrows,
and prefer
exotic vegetarian dishes to good, solid,
stick-to-your-ribs kind of food.
she'd be walking, living, eating,
and breathing virtue. would willingly
and sheepishly follow my lead and
take care of home and family needs.
my folks.
if they were given an inch, they'd take

a whole ten damn miles
and have me and the wife
taking a cruise to hawaii or
down the Pacific coast of Mexico
on the love boat,
after ten or fifteen years on the job.
the way they see it, you may not be
quite as young, but count your blessings
and be thankful that you're able. this father
and mother of mine, they'd love to see me
kicked back with a nice, expensive ride,
a three-hundred and fifty thousand dollar pad,
another four-hundred grand
in several different banks, income property,
and a big fat juicy retirement check waiting
in the wings. most
of all,
they want me to be happy.

Aunt Lola's Take On Black History

it was a labor of total futility convincin
dear dear Aunt Lola
that black folks had indeed been brought
from Africa and had built empires
like Songhai and Mali
where great cities flourished and centers
of learning like Timbuktu abounded for centuries

in fact
you'd be too through and completely blown away
for callin black folks
anythang other than negroes
accordin to dear dear Aunt Lola negroes came from some
remote desolate island in the mid-Atlantic
right below the equator called Negros
and it said so in both sets of encyclopedias
that had been in the family since 1887
when her great-grandpa bought them from a salesman
travlin through their small rural Alabama town

tryin to discuss the wherefores therefores
howfores and whyfores of the information
distorted by some sho nuff lyin connivin racists
in the Encyclopedia Amerikkkana
would make you a low down dirty no good triflin
nigguh
who was doomed to dwell in the darkness of ignorance
and die

and burn in the eternal fires of damnation
for bein so ungrateful and god forsakenly uppity
after all if it wasn't for good upstanding white folks
all these fool nigguhs runnin around
talkin about all this unity revoltin and controllin
the community
would still be back on Negros starvin
half naked and "ignant" as ever

For My Cousin, De Mayor

strange
even in our closeness & tightness
we hardly feel
each other's presence
not even facin
each other
2 tables away
in this downtown
Berkeley restaurant
2 blk men
young
caught
in the senility
of gooey chocolate sundaes
you a politician
me a poet
strange
the adjectives of existence
don't just bring recognition
& attract notice
they also make
great distances
between
2
hearts

Sunday Morning

for Rev. & Mrs. Robert D. Hill

Every time I've come back to this corner,
at 12th and Adeline,
where Taylor United Methodist Church
sits cloud white and majestically
against a misted turquoise sky,
the hush, quietness, and stillness
have never ceased to amaze and humble me.

Yes! In all my years
of coming here to take refuge
away from the fast track of my madness,
this hush, this quiet, this stillness
of a Sunday morning
puts this wandering temple of the Lord
back in its proper order,
where layers of dust have collected
and the altar of the soul that lives here
left in so much disarray.

What flora sprouts from the hats,
what fauna
snuggles around the shoulders of
the church sisters
draws me back to the fold this morning?
Will the words of a hymn
touch a chord in my heart this morning?
Will I find a metaphor hidden in this morning's

scripture reading
or an ultimate truth in the pastor's sermon
to start the wheels of righteousness turning
in this big, rock hard head of mine
this morning?

Nothing is given and nothing is gained
when the journeys home are only brief flights
from the world's horrors,
unless, of course, you've come to stay.

An Urgent Visual Message from the Poet

A ss

I n

D eep

S hit

How I Started Writing Poetry

How I Started Writing Poetry

At the age of fourteen I was what Richard Pryor over a decade later would call "going for bad" or what my Southern-bred folks said was "smellin' your pee." That is, I had cultivated a facade of daring-do, hip, cool, con man bravado so prevalent among adolescent males in West Oakland. I "talked that talk and walked that walk" most parents found downright despicable. In their minds these were dress rehearsals of fantasies that were Popsicles that would melt and evaporate under the heat of blazing hot realities. And there I was doing the pimp limp and talking about nothing profound or sustaining. All I wanted to do was project that image of being forever cool like Billy Boo, who used to wear three T-shirts , two slipover sweaters and a thick Pendleton shirt tucked neatly in his khaki or black Ben Davidsons to give everybody the impression that he was buffed (muscle bound) and definitely not to be messed with. Cool. Real cool. Standing in front of the liquor store on 35th and San Pablo sipping white port and lemon juice, talking smack by the boatloads until some real hoodlum from Campbell Village or Harbor Homes with the *real* biceps, the shonuff triceps and sledgehammer fists beat the shirt, both sweaters, the T-shirts and pants right off of Billy Boo's weak, bony body.

Herbert Hoover Junior High, the school I attended, was considered one of three toughest in Oakland at that time. It was a dirty, gray, forbidding looking place where several fights would break out every day. There was a joke going around that a mother, new to the city, mistook it for the Juvenile Detention Center that was further down in West Oakland on 18th and Poplar right across the street from DeFremery Park.

During my seventh-grade year there were constant referrals to the principal's office for any number of infractions committed either in Miss Okamura's third-period music class or Mrs. George's sixth-period math class in the basement where those of us with behavioral problems and assumed learning disabilities were sent. It was also around this time that Harvey Hendricks, my main running buddy, took it upon himself to hip me to everything he thought I needed to know about sex while we were doing a week's detention in Mrs. Belasco's art class for capping on "them steamer trunks" or "suitcases" under her eyes. As we sat there, supposedly writing "I will not insult the teacher" one hundred times, Harvey would draw pictures of huge tits and vaginas, while telling me how to rap, kiss and jump off in some twanks and stroke. Told me that the pimples on my face were "pussy bumps," and that I'd better start getting some trim or end up just like Crater Face Jerome with the big, nasty-looking quarter-size pus bumps all over his face

Though my behavior left a lot to be desired, I managed to earn some fairly decent grades. I loved history, art and English, and somehow managed to work my way up from special education classes to college prep courses by the time I reached ninth grade, my last year at Hoover. But by then I had become a full-fledged little thug, and had been suspended—and damn near expelled—quite a few times for going to knuckle city at the drop of a hat for any real or imagined reason. And what an efficient thief I'd become. This was something I'd picked up from my cousins, R.C. and Danny, when I started hanging out with them on weekends in San Francisco's Haight-Ashbury. We'd steal clothes, records, liquor, jewelry— anything for the sake of magnifying to the umpteenth degree that image of death-defying manhood and to prove I was indeed a budding Slick Draw McGraw. Luckily, I was never caught, arrested and hauled off to Juvenile Hall or the California Youth Authority like so many of the guys I ran with.

Probably through pressure from my parents and encouragement from my teachers and counselors, I forced myself to start thinking about pursuing a career after graduation from high school, which was three years away. Reaching into the grab bag of professional choices, I decided I wanted to become a physician, since doctors were held in such high esteem, particularly in an Afro-American community like West Oakland. I'd gotten it in my head that I wanted to be a plastic surgeon, no less, because I liked working with my hands and found science intriguing. Then something strange happened.

Maybe it was the continuous violence, delinquency and early pregnancies that made those Oakland Unified School District administrators (more than likely after some consultation with psychologists) decide to put a little Freudian theory to practical use. Just as I was grooving, really getting into this fantastic project in fourth-period art class, I was called up to the teacher's desk and handed a note and told to report to a classroom downstairs on the first floor. What had I done this time? Was it because I snatched Gregory Jones' milkshake during lunch a couple of days ago and gulped it down, savoring every drop like an old loathsome suck-egg dog, and feeling no pain as the chump, big as he was, stood there and cried? And Mr. Foltz, the principal, was known to hand out mass suspensions. Sometimes fifteen, twenty, twenty-five people at a time. But when I entered the classroom, there sat this tall, gangly, goofy-looking white woman who wore her hair unusually long for that time, had thick glasses and buckteeth like the beaver on the Ipana Toothpaste commercials. Some of the roughest, toughest kids that went to Hoover were in there. Especially big old mean, ugly Martha Dupree who was known to knock out boys, girls, and teachers when she got the urge. If Big Martha asked you for a last-day-of-school kiss, you'd better give it up or make an appointment with your dentist.

When Miss Nettelbeck finally got our attention, she announced that this was a creative writing class that would meet twice a week. Creative writing? What the hell is creative writing a couple of us asked. She explained that it was a way to express what was on your mind, and a better way of getting something off of your chestthan beating up your fellow students. Then she read a few poems to us and passed out some of that coarse school-issue lined paper and told us to write about something we liked, disliked, or really wanted.

What I wanted to know was, did it have to be one of "them pomes." "If that's how you want to express yourself, Reginald," she said. So I started racking my brain, trying to think about what I liked, didn't like and what I really wanted. Well, I liked football, track and Gayle Johnson, who would turn her cute little "high yella" nose up in total disgust everytime I tried to say something to her.

I couldn't stand the sight—not even the thought—of old monkey-face Martha. And what I really wanted was either a '57 Buick Roadmaster or a '56 Chevy with mag wheels and tuck 'n' roll seats that dropped in the front like the ones I'd seen older dudes like Mack's brother, Skippy, riding around in. Naw, I told myself, I couldn't get away with writing about things like that. I might get into some more trouble, and Big Martha would give me a thorough asskicking for writing something about mashing her face in some dough and baking me some gorilla cookies. Who'd ever heard of a poem about cars? One thing I really liked was the ocean. I guess that was in my blood because my father was then a Master Chief Steward in the Navy, and, when I was younger, would take me aboard ships docked at Hunter's Point and Alameda. I loved the sea so much that I would sometimes walk from my house on Market and W. MacArthur all the way to the Berkeley Pier or take a bus to Ocean Beach in San Francisco whenever I wasn't up to no good. So I wrote:

> I sit on a rock
> watching

> the evening tide
> come in.
> The green waves travel
> with the wind.
> They seem to carry
> a message of
> warning or plea
> from the dimensions
> of time and distance.

When I gave it to Miss Nettelbeck, she read it and told me it was good for a first attempt at writing poetry, and since there was still some time left in the period, I should go back to my seat and write something else. Damn! These teachers never gave you any kind of slack, no matter what you did and how well you did it. Now, what else could I think of to write about? How about a tribute to Miss Bobby, the neighborhood drag queen, who'd been found carved up like a Christmas turkey a week ago? Though me, Harvey and Mack used to crack jokes about "her" giving up the boodie, we still liked and respected "her" because she would give you five or six dollars to run an errand to the cleaners or the store, never tried to hit on you, and would get any of the other "girls" straight real quick if they even said you were cute or something. So I wrote:

> Bring on the hustlers
> in Continental suits
> and alligator shoes.
> Let ladies of the night

> In short, tight dresses
> And spiked heels enter.
> We are gathered here
> To pay tribute to
> The Queen of Drag.
> What colorful curtains
> And rugs!
> Look at the stereo set
> And the clothes in the closet.
> On the bed, entangled
> In a bloody sheet,
> Is that elegant one
> Of ill repute
> But good carriage
> Oh yes! There
> Was none like her.
> The Queen of Drag.

When she read that one, I just knew Miss Nettelbeck would immediately write a referral and have me sent back upstairs. But she liked it and said I was precocious for someone at such an innocent age. Innocent? When was I ever innocent? I was guilty of just about everything I was accused of doing. Like, get your eyes checked, baby. And what was precocious? Was it something weird? Did it mean I was queer like Miss Bobby? Was I about to go to snap city like poor Donny Moore had a year ago when he suddenly got up and started jacking off in front of Mr. Lee's history class? What did this woman, who looked and dressed like one of them beatniks I'd seen one night on *East Side, West*

Side, mean? My Aunt Audrey's boyfriend, Joe, told me beatniks were smart and used a lot of big words like precocious so nobody could understand what they were talking about. Had to be something bad. This would mess with me for the rest of the week if I didn't ask her what she meant. So I did, and she told me it meant that I knew about things somebody my age didn't usually know about. Wow! That could only mean that I was "hip to the lip." But I already knew that.

For some reason I wasn't running up and down the streets with the fellas much anymore. Harvey would get bent out of shape everytime I'd tell him I had something else to do. I had to be turning punkish or seeing some girl I was too chinchy to introduce him to. This also bothered my mother because she kept telling me I was going to ruin my eyes if I didn't stop reading so much; and what was that I spent all my spare time writing in a manila notebook? Was I keeping a diary or something? Only girls kept diaries, and people may start thinking I was one "them sissy mens" if I didn't stop. Even getting good grades and citizenship and making the honor roll didn't keep her off of my case. But I kept right on reading and writing, looking forward to Miss Nettelbeck's class twice a week. I stopped fighting, too. But I was still roguish as ever. Instead of raiding Rogers Men's Shop, Smith's and Flagg Brothers' Shoes, I was stealing books by just about every poet and writer Miss Nettelbeck read to the class. That's how I started writing poetry.

What It Be Like

What You See Ain't What You Are

for Jaleel Atif Haynes, Phyl's Son

it wouldve been a real real
groove   when I moved thru those
years of discovery after
discovery   wonder after
wonder   to sit before the
toxic beam of the tv set & see
Black Bart hijack Wells Fargo
gold shipments on old California roads or
wish i was there when my
ace boon John threw a wang-dang
-doodle in the big house after the
massa & the missus went away to
some place good home folks call
Philly-me-Jinks*
it wouldve been real
nice to sit in front of the
tv set & watch big bad
Shango streak across the
sky on seven bolts of lightning or dig
mighty Horus put another
whipping on some
square name Seth
it wouldve been outta sight & a pure
delight to just know that
Marie Laveau was hiding somewhere in my
bedroom walls   came out at

night when everybody slept   told me
strange & wonderful things &
gave me a gris-gris bag all my very own
it wouldve been great to
imagine riding with the
Divine Horsemen of the heavens & be real
tight with old slick Legba &
Ogun the warrior god
it wouldve been mighty
fine to see all of this in the
cold & hateful stare of the
tv set
but it was even
finer & warmer
nicer & sweeter to
listen to my
grandma   mamafromwaydownhome
tell me how Brer Rabbit put one or
two over on Brer Fox & Brer Bear
sing songs & tell more
tales of real folks & heroes that
moved thru her days
thru her years
her life

*from the African-American folktale
"Massa Takes A Trip."

The Silent Songwriter Of Our Apocalypse

for James Washington Blake

He's got a high-stepping Texas Hop
in his walk,
an old-time bottleneck blues in the
way he talks & countless records of
events & unheard of songs in the
expression on his ageless face.
Collages of gutbucket truths &
revelations persist in his
endless gaze.
He's the silent songwriter
of our Apocalypse.
He keeps a Big John de Conqueror
root in his hip pocket & a
lodestone hidden
neatly away in his vest.

The golden radiance of his smile
dances past trembling veils & travels
far beyond the comprehension of
reddish clouds in the hot pinkness of
warm evening skies.
Even in the dim blue light of
creation's flame,
it shines.

He's the silent songwriter of our
Apocalypse.
He keeps a Big John de Conqueror root
in his hip pocket & a lodestone
hidden neatly away in his vest
right beneath an old gold watch
on a tarnished silver chain,
this powerful composer of the
syncopated ebony tune.

SONG OF FIRE

Like Ogun, father of iron,
who went from the sight of men,
way up into the heights of
Oke Ori to make weapons
the world had never seen,
Eric Dolphy ascended into
the mountain of his wisdom
to create music,
sweet, sweet music the world
had never heard.
Sounds that've endured
all the deprivation & degradation
of this ice age
that lingers here.
This age, this age
that has brought so much death,
so much sorrow, so many tears
to our mothers' eyes.

Armed with knowledge
that too many sounds, words & pictures
move,
pass through our minds,
go up into the air, never to return,
the Iron Man forged
musical spears of fire

as sharp as the Sun Bird's beak.
Flaming spears too strong.
Flaming spears too swift.
Flaming spears too much
for closed-eared, empty-headed,
short-sighted listeners whose minds
went out to lunch and
never came back.

This son, this son,
this son of Ogun, who
like his brother Bird before him,
who like his brother Prez before him,
handed the tools of his craft
to his brother Trane,
saying,
"Take my hammer and my anvil,
but don't tell the cap'n."

Ramses' Dance*

for DeLeon, Malcolm, Salim, and Al-Batim, and in memory of D.T.

Entering the forest he moves not the grass;
Entering the water he makes not a ripple. **

Ramses as dancer-magician moves soundlessly
unseen slick as grease, fast as a
breeze that swoops by you in a quick flash on a fall day
along the always endlessly changing shore
as the Sun, great disc, eye of RA peeps all 360 degrees of
the planet beneath yellow and orange
rays on this new day for new steps, flight patterns
ripening here
               here
                             here
now
               now
                             now
all
               all
                             all
the planet
               planet
                             planet
earth
               earth
                             earth
Ramses as man, as spirit

moves along the shore and runs into a dancing Conjure
Woman,
Shady Lady of hot summer days, warm spring nights.
Skin, hair, body deep moving ageless rivers and oceans;
thick forest and vast, never ending plains.
Movements silent, swift like a bird gliding with the
                                    wind's course.
Ramses and the Conjure Woman as one dancer-magician
The tribes as one dancer,
as one dance,
move with the fast Shady Couple along the shore
to the endless sounds of drums, horns, and natural
rhythms
in Damballah's image.   Moving from blue velvet night
into red velvet dawn.
Ramses and the Conjure Woman and the tribes
                                as one DANCE
suck in the clean, cool, moist air
  let it out,
and become like a flock of birds in clear, open sky
and dance
        as one Dance on this new day
                                    for new
steps
that be for real.

*A choreopoem choreographed and performed by Elendar
Barnes and Shirley Brown in February, 1971.

**from the *ZENRIN*.

A Lesson In Aesthetics

when somebody
tells me
that i'm
supposed to
write this way
& live my life
that way
or the other,
i tell
them that we
may be
using the
same airline,
but our
flight numbers
are different.

Bro. Radio & Me

Bro. Radio & Me

my radio lives on the large shelf,
right above the bed.   talk about a
funny little sucker.   very bourgeois
(I would even go as far as to say dicty). won't accept
nothing less than the best.
lives solely on a choice, highly nutritional diet
of good, sweet, refreshing, fingerpopping
sound.   the
wisdom of rounded reeds, piercing brass, crashing
percussion, steady bass & well tuned piano
keys creep through his mind.
considers himself the primary, major authority
on the subject of sound.   can expound
extensively on any one genre.   always rises
to the occasion.   claims to have written
volumes & volumes & volumes on music's
life, culture,
                philosophy & religion.   says
that there is only one truly healthy sound.   & please
don't dispute his word if you don't want
your feelings hurt.
swears he comes from some
big, rich, important family named Zenith
in the Midwest.   came this way in '62.
can't say it's not true, but
I remember seeing him hanging out at this

pawnshop downtown L.A. on Main St. between
4th & 5th hustling dimes for new tubes.

Bro. Radio's New Occupation

today, my radio told
me that he was "godsent."   that is, a bonafide,
gen-u-ine, hope-to-die messenger of "the Lord, God, Himself
in person." said the spirit speaks through
two gaping holes in his right speaker every Sunday at
4 p.m.
serious as shit on your shoes about it, too.
square business.   professed to have a family tree
four days older than air & heavier than
eleven elephant rumps (now, that's what he
said).   started telling me how his extension
cord reached way back before the beginning
of Egyptian civilization.   said some long-beaked,
bird-faced dude named Thoth was his forefather. stone
blue blood.   knew that crazy noise box was
about to flip (& I mean completely lose it) when he claimed to
have "visited" this life a couple hundred times as an
amoeba, prophet, poet, musician, whore, gangster, cockroach & other
assorted things. then he hit me up for a
10 &
a 20. when I refused, he
threatened to put a freeze on the sound if I didn't
oblige.   said his new occupation doesn't
rate social security or fringe benefits.

Radio In Love

that weird radio put me in his
most confidential confidence this afternoon.
confessed a flaming, red hot, passionate
love for the beautiful component set that lives in the next
room.

said that he would like to know her name.
doesn't matter if nothing happens.   just a kind
hello would be fine.
                              admitted imagining
the smooth feel of her deep
                          mahogany finish.
has complete orgasms every time he thinks about the
symmetry of her delicate design.

the very mention of her 8-speaker system
ignites his innermost desires.   wants to caress
her speakers, lick her knobs, roll on her turntable
                        & connect his FM tuner
                                to hers.
asked me if I knew how much
                      she
was worth.   wants a sound financial
relationship, as well as
                          an emotional one,
because he needs a place to lay when times
get hard.

Bro. Radio's Paranoia

lately,
my radio has become quite dis-
turbed about what he calls my
infidelity where our friendship is concerned.
thinks I've copped an attitude.   says the
AM/FM radio who lives in my car is
the cause of it all.
                        doesn't trust car
radios, anyway.   thinks they are a waste of
good juice.   says he smells the "lingering stench"
                        of an illicit relationship." feels
I've acquired a dreadful air
of vanity about myself.   doesn't like the
way I comb my hair & thinks
shaving every other day is too often. says it shows
signs of a nasty disposition.   insists that
I stop keeping bad company.
that is, I shouldn't hang out with radios that
run on batteries.   parasites.   leeches.   free-
loaders.   will leave you standing in the cold
                        when your shit gets
raggedy.   thinks I should let him
run with me. says he knows 39 different ways
to party at the expense of others.

Bro. Radio & My Kind Of Women

my radio tells me that he
doesn't particularly dig any of
                 my lady friends.　says he
sees no obvious signs of "intellectual
                       or spiritual depth."
thinks they lack dignity, positive
                   values & the basic moral
standards.　especially since they associate
with the "likes" of me or
someone like me.　can only visualize
me as a "rare breed of dog."　mostly
because I have the most "primitive, grotesque
methods of gratifying" my "base,
carnal desires."　says my "lowdown
lustful ways" can only be surpassed
by those of the "most negligent life forms."
all of my women friends are of some kind of "fanatical,
decadent, perverted persuasion" because they
can be persuaded by & attracted to the
"lewd designs" of my "very soul."　has
visions of them lapping up my vital energies
like "a host of vampires."　thinks I
should start spending my weekends alone.
anyway, the moans, groans & sighs always
make him contemplate jacking off.

Bro. Radio's Protest

today, my radio became fiercely
              "perplexed" about sharing his
shelf with a friend's radio that
      has taken up temporary
residence in "our fair abode" until
my friend gets settled somewhere

                                          else.

doesn't like it because the other radio
                        has an extra
speaker & is plugged into the same socket.
thinks it's trying
to cramp his style because it's
tuned to the same station.   has
                  hinted at a possible
homicide whenever the lights go out.   is threatening
to push it off the shelf.   feels it's his "revolutionary
duty" because he sees the other radio as a
              colonizer/oppressor that takes
up too much space & requires too much
juice. just because it's from
Berkeley (& happens to be a "he" instead of a
"she"), he fears my friend's radio may carry something
"contagious."   says Berkeley is a filthy place, anyway.
says he doesn't trust a radio that
can pick up foreign stations because
he suspects him—my friend's radio—of conspiring to
overthrow "our great room under one roof, one person,
one radio & the landlord."

Gettin' Some...

A Kite Poem For You

>   you
>   are life
>   make & keep
>   beauty & warmth
>   love & hold
>   your arm
>   out
>   &
>   p
>   u
>   l
>   l
>   me
>   i
>   n

untitled

my woman is sleeping
through the evening.
I slip on a wool sweater & step
outside for air into
a San Francisco autumn,
as slow Pacific winds
knock yellow & brown leaves
from trees growing, breaking through
weather smoothed, manhandled
sidewalks.
it's nice out here
in the quiet coolness
& aloneness
on this street facing
our building.
inside, where my lady love rests,
the plants are strong & green,
dishes need washing, clothes put away,
books & albums reshelved,
papers corrected,
poems & stories written,
money made & love saved
in the swiftness of
another quick decade running,
passing through the eyes
of these houses.

The X-Lovers

she calls.
he picks up the receiver.
he ask her how she been
doin and she says fine
and ask him how he
been doin.
he says fine and mentions
that it's been over a year.
she agrees and says she
misses him at times.
he asks her what she's been into
and she says she's
been goin to school, workin,
takin guitar lessons and
chantin.
then she asks him what he been
doin and he talks about
work, exercisin and hangin
out.
he asks her to come over.
she says yeah!
she's there in 30 minutes.
they sit in his room,
drink some wine, smoke a
joint, listen to some sides and
talk.
then they embrace, hug, caress
and kiss and kiss and kiss.

bust some slobs like
there ain't gonna be no tomorrow.
he strokes her back and she strokes
his.
he runs his fingers through
her hair.
he kisses her eyes.
he kisses her cheeks.
he bites her ears.
he moves his hands towards
them big old luscious
breasts, and he's almost
there, ready for the down-stroke,
when she brushes his hand
away gently and
says,
"umh! umh! I just wanted
to see if the feelin was
still there, honey, and
it ain't"

405 Scott Street

pushin a hard forty, ten years away
from a half century of livin,
he down shifts from third into second
and hooks a right off Fulton onto Scott,
down the hill, towards McAllister,
where that apartment buildin
now conjures up enough strength
to withstand the bombardment
of another quick decade
comin at it like an angry, irrational mob
bent on its total destruction.
he knows it well
because in that same buildin, on the same floor,
right across the hall from each other,
seven years apart, he'd loved two women.
yes, as a grad student at twenty-three,
when the only thing he was drivin
was that pair of Adidas—or them Frye boots
when the weather was bad—it was Vera.
long, tall, fine high yella drink of water
Vera with the flamin red, sky high 'fro.
Vera, four or five years older,
who was gettin down with a movement
for a people oppressed and hungry for change.
and oh! the motion of that vast ocean
when them lean, ripe, creamy banana legs
were spread out beneath him,
thrustin upwards so hard, it damn near

knocked him clean on out that fourth floor
bedroom window one wintry night
two weeks before finals.
vera. cool drink of lemonade vera,
gettin down with the people, the movement,
and him.
then at thirty, when that buildin
had begun deterioratin so suddenly,
Connye was there in the apartment across the hall
where a daughter's curses and disrespect
for her mother had flowed so profusely
seven years before.
all six feet, two inches,
one-hundred and eighty pounds of sweet,
delectable chocolate goodness there to listen,
comfort, and drive him into uncharted realms
of ecstasy with gargantuan number fifty
double d's, good, skilled head,
and tons and tons of Iowa farm girl passion
every Wednesday or Thursday night
on schedule
when all that desperate desire, that just couldn't
wait,
came tumblin down out of both of them.
no matter the time, he'd
somehow get there from way out in the mission
for just one more taste of that chocolate
that melted into his heart
as well as in his mouth.

Cheeseburgers

in the constant
nonstop moments of our urgency
in this,
the rush hour of history,
our desires and lusts
for the good things in life
are cheeseburgers
sizzling and popping
on the front burner
of our lives.

love is
a good, fresh, wholesome
melody of vegetables
steaming slowly on the back burner
of our needs
until it's ready
to nourish and sustain us.

Shoulda-Coulda-Woulda

for Betty (Bogard) Jackson

This is a shoulda-coulda-woulda thing
we have for each other,
regretting
yet resolving
all those moments not seized
when we hung tight,
ace-boons
burning up the curbs
up and down Berkeley and all over Oakland
before we would
sizzle into the City across the Bay.
Two madcap conspirators,
this Taurus woman and Scorpio man
conjured up the parties and big fun
in places and spaces
where nothing was even remotely
happening.
We breathed life
into the deadness of slow Friday
and Saturday nights
that dripped honey-sweetened music
and colored every urban
nook, cranny, and crevice
graced with our mischievous,
ethereal presence.
Forever chocolate buddies,
we now wonder

what it shoulda-coulda-woulda
been like
had we become lovers.

10/20/94

Funky Truths and Realities

Good Times & No Bread

for Babs Gonzales

we move very fast & smoothly
thru serious cities & states
down with the common cold or the
flu
we may not have the bread &
we may be scufflin hard hard hard
but we got all the fun
cause our colors got sounds
& our sounds got colors
spaced out thru & beyond time
our immortal images & spirits
dance space dances
from way back
in ancient tribal rites for
some good & powerful Loa
like Papa Legba
always on his job at the gate
all the way to some of them mean
nowtime steps & mystical variations
we be pullin off on
abstract invaders of
the apocalypse out to
snap the lifelines to our
visions as we move at
safe speeds
down highways

tightly sprinkled with signs that
tell us where & when to go
but our elders taught us the
signs
taught us
right from left
round from square
on from off
here from there
we are afro-spacemen travelin in
view of the mind's eye
psychic hitmen ready to
melt the mental ice
celestial custodians who
brush away the spirit's frost
circuit riders
takin back streets to the
music & good times in these
articulate chess playin
trump holdin
cities & states

The Movement

Thangs weren't always like this.
We were circuit riders of Garvey's whirlwind,
workin the rhythms of blues drenched streets,
jazz soaked nightclubs and gatherins
of houngans and necramancers committed to struggle,
breathin the fire of Malcolm's words.

Martin Luther King, Jr. Way was Grove Street,
and no children stood on corners
speakin the language of doom and hawkin
the wares of self-doubt and destruction.

Fillmore was alive with the comins and goins and doins
of a people dancin
across collard green floors and holdin up cornbread
walls
under buttermilk skies,
pawin, clawin, dreamin, schemin, screamin. . .
gettin up, standin up, and flyin, dyin, cryin, connivin
their way towards newer tomorrows.

Good brothas and sistas on the speedboat
of revolution, our sights set on this thang
called freedom.

Thangs weren't always dismal and dank like this.
We were cosmic griots takin the point,
searchin infinite perimeters of sights and sounds
from the funky four corners of existence,

talkin smack by the boatloads and gettin one up
on the would-be grafters of our dreams,
slippin and slidin through concrete bayous
in urban undergrowth,
the bloodhounds of oppression, repression,
and suppression
snappin and bayin at the iridescence of our heels.
Some of us drank gallons and gallons of Red Mountain
or shortneck after shortneck of Ripple
under the harsh glow of red and blue party lights,
and held tight to women blacker than forty midnights,
suddenly beautiful,
gettin the R-E-S-P-E-C-T and do rightness
Aretha demanded in that brand new bag
James Brown shouted and hollered into our thoughts.

Thangs weren't always crazy like this.

Incarcerated in the desolate barnyards of Amerikkka,
we were fast and slick in the way we saw ourselves.
Cutesie tootsie roosters wearin our crowns
a good fifty degrees to the side,
and laid, sprayed, and ready to get paid
in plummage of silk and satin,
we kept the hawks of our misery confused and
perplexed
beyond cocaine and cognac tainted perspectives.

We were keepers of the eagle's eye view,
on the watch out for the cutthroats of reason
and the backstabbers of sanity

on these long, windin and twistin highways and by-
ways,
bookin midnight flights of fancy
on the music of Trane, Albert, and Pharoah,
the teachins of Fanon, Mao, Che, and Huey,
and the muses of Baraka, Sonia, Askia and Larry,
tryin to get back home to Ditty-Wah-Ditty
in a nick of time to call winners
and cash in all the chips
in this game of chance called life.

When They Came To Take Him

in memory of Robert Garner

when they came for him,
it wasn't the gentility of his
tastefully painted, neat single-level
Victorian house tucked away
in a decent neighborhood
that they saw.
when they came to take him,
it wasn't the meticulously
restored vintage Jaguar in the garage
or the shiny MG parked
in the driveway that they
took note of.
when they had come
to subdue him, it wasn't
the aesthetic choice of furniture,
original paintings, carvings,
and prints
they looked on in awe at.
when they entered his space,
uninvited, to force on him
their lopsided wills, it
wasn't the impressive collection of books
that covered one whole wall or the
careful selection of jazz classics they came
to train their cold, insensitive
gazes on.

when they had come to
confront him, it wasn't the
conservative tweed, chic tie and handmade shoes
he wore they came all dressed in blue
to out flaunt.
when they had come to exercise the powers
vested in them to uproot him
from his own being, it wasn't the master of arts
degree, secure job with a bank,
and superb fiction and criticism
he wrote that
they took into consideration that morning
on the last day in may.
when they came to capture his spirit
and erase his vision,
it wasn't the intelligence in his eyes,
the ready pride in his face, and the gentleness
in his voice that they wanted to see.
no.
all they saw was that he was black,
believed armed and dangerous,
and resisting arrest when they fired a .12 gauge
riot pump, point-blank,
dead off in his chest.

Prediction*

in the western hemisphere of my mind,
cities rot from the inside out,
from the outside in,
like carcasses of dead cattle
on hot, dry, windswept,
once lush savannas.

in the way out west of my consciousness,
jelly bean munching gargoyles
pour salt on the festering wounds
of the sun-kissed masses.

in the western sector of my thoughts,
sulfur breath demons
prepare for some unholy
crusade under
Latin American and Caribbean skies
where mangoes, bananas, guavas,
and genipas grow,
and all the birds of paradise
sing the true meaning
of imagination.

*This poem was written almost 2 years before the U.S. invasion of Grenada on October 25, 1983.

She Tries: Reflections On A Student's Homework Assignment

she's 18
but you would swear
she's 12. tiny tidy & sweet.
hasn't missed a class
in two semesters. is
never late. always
there right on time
waiting in 7:45 a.m. damp
gray Monday morning downtown Oakland
fog. pays good attention.
takes all the tests.
attempts all the assignments & still
reads at a second grade
level.
the song of her
heavy-lipped/gapped-tooth
cackle leaps & bounces
off the puzzled scowls
on the decaying masks
of modern learning
methods.
took the class
again because she says
she's learning a lot &
thinks I'm crazy.
even brought her
mother out in the rain

to see
the show.
she tries.
correcting
yesterday's assignments
I read/heard that metaphor/tune
which is her heartbeat
which is our history
burned/forged into
3 sentences on
school issue line paper
in big hurried scribbled block letters:
1. Mr. Lockett is a good read
   and, writting teacher.
2. me and, my firend with to
   Laney College School.
3. I going to have a baby on
   July 23 and I going to miss
   you Mr. Lockett because you
   is a very good teacher.

The Terminator

this homey in my class.
loud yellow baseball cap
pulled waaaaaaaaay down
over matted, jet black blue
ocean waves and earphones
hooked up to a matching
yellow Walkman radio
hidden in the inside pocket
of a black leather Raiders jacket.
feeling good behind large
smoke tinted shades.
high on indica and crack
rolled into a grimmie,
he rides his mountain bike
in a continuous circle
around the block during
both his fifteen minute breaks
and the entire lunch hour.
this week,
he's found himself another
momentary niche.
some immediate gratification thing
that'll last for
about only a week.
maybe a month.
has awarded himself a detailed,
hand printed certificate of
death defying manhood,
complete with personal logo.

calls himself "the terminator."
another lost wanderer
caught in the padded cell of
some media spawned
image of awesome masculinity
that's going to keep him
cruising
in that same small circle,
leaving no mental aftertaste.

Pamela: A Case of Extreme Abuse

sweet as she can be. petite.
just turned eighteen. red streaked
doodoo braids. could improve her reading,
writing and math if she'd just
apply herself more. never stops
grinning and is constantly talking
in class when she's suppose
to be doing her work. it's that big, loud,
sarcastic mouth of hers
that writes checks her tiny, itty bitty ass
can't cash. an ultimate object of abuse,
she's the class whipping post. all she
has to do is be there, and presto!
it's fuck with Pamela time.
her baby's father keeps his foot
off in her ass, mostly on g.p.
his cousin accuses
her of fucking another homey
while her man was doing
some serious vacationing up in Stockton,
courtesy
of the California Youth Authority,
and kicks her in both shins
whenever the mood hits him. her
mother rejects her, her p.o.
denies her, and the program counselor
downright despises and hates her. one
of the fellas in her remedial reading and writing class
found a straight razor. had to

try it out on something or somebody.
cut a gash down the palm of her left hand
long, tall, and continuously.
rushed her to S.F. General.
blood and tears all over her blouse,
all over my jeans and penny loafers.
waited an hour and a half before she
was called. took seventeen stitches,
and she comes out of the emergency room
grinning.

A Child Of Our Revolution

for Judy Juanita in Jersey

the years have not been kind to him.
nothing gained for all that's
been given and taken. how old
should he be now? twenty-four, twenty-five, . . .twenty-
six?
Little John who dug
hanging with all the brothers and sisters
in the movement out at S.F. State.
fast talking, chubby little kid
straight from the projects
in the Fillmore. hip little
nine year old
we saw as
a raw reflection of what we only played
at being, walking that walk,
talking bushels of trash, and keeping up
a ruckus all over
campus. primed with neurotic illusions
of the revolution that was just
around the corner,
the sky was the limit, and it was
open season on anybody or
anything that even
seemed opposed
to the struggle. bad little
old John. wild
as an adolescent leopard cub

turned loose at a staid,
high society cocktail
party. little john
all grown up hard, reminiscing about
the haps out at State
way back then. finally
starting that eternal game of catch-up
in the reading class
I teach. Little John no longer
the mischievous boy we let
run free. Little John
now a man with definite needs,
holding firmly to the ideas
we stuffed into his head
when we should've also been
teaching him how to read.

Occupational Lycanthropy

(A Variation On A Theme By Lorenzo Thomas)

he's worked in that same office,
scrunched up in this same desolate corner,
riveted to that same raggedy desk,
ten years too long,
revolving around the somebodies and somethings,
never letting them revolve around him.

on holidays, his days off,
or on his vacation, he finds himself
halfway down the freeway
before he remembers it's not a work day.

he can't remember where he's from.
he's forgotten who he is.
he's not sure where he's going.

since his supervisor bit him in the jugular vein
of his self-consciousness on the last full moon,
he's felt all funny inside.

look!
his toe nails and fingernails
have grown long and curled inwardly along
the cuticles.
watch it!
his nose is getting snoutish and blue steel cold
to the touch.

oh no!
fangs are starting to protrude
from his upper and lower jaws.
frothy, rabid saliva is dribbling down the corners
of his mouth.
believe me when I tell you his ears are now pointed
and brownish-grey hair has sprouted out
all over his body.
his eyes have gone from being big and bright
to being slanted and blood shot.
has this sudden urge to pounce on his coworkers.
sees his love ones
in the five cornered stars in the palms
of his lethal hands.
they've all started to pack pistols
loaded with silver bullets and give him all the space
he can handle.

he's found comraderie among his supervisors
and, of course, his boss who, of course,
turned everybody out.
his days and nights are spent running with the pack
and howling at the moon
after a few wolfgang stouts
over at the wolfskeller bar & grill.

he's running with the pack.
he's achieved the american dream.
he's running with the pack
with whom he's made a pact.

all he cares about is howling at the full moon
with the rest of the pack.

Superstition

by the time we'd moved in,
they'd already staked out their territory
in the garden,
behind the garage. an
unspoken truce between us;
I don't throw rocks at them,
and they stay out of the way
when I come trudging
through the backyard for any number
of reasons unknown
even to me.
these cats. this family of black cats.
male, female and two kittens
kicking back where the stringbeans
have grown too tough and fibrous
for consumption,
or soaking up some sun over
where the okra, tomatoes and corn
are just right for a decent succotash.
all these black cats
living off the fat of the property
I'm renting and criss-crossing
my path a zillion times
a day. is it really bad luck
if a black cat crosses your path?
as city born, city spoiled children of good, country-
bred folk,
we turned seven times

in a circle to keep the bad luck monkeys
off our backs. I'd stay higher
than a Georgia Pine
if I turned
seven times in a circle
everytime one of these cool, collective cats
crossed my path.
could this be why an uninsured driver
backed into my parked car
the other day?
is this why I'm late
getting to work everyday, no matter
how early I leave?
these black cats may figure in the episode
of not one, but two pulled hamstrings
while out jogging last week.
all my friends have stopped calling
and coming by.
think I'll pack my black jogging outfit,
take a flight
to D.C., and dart back and forth
in front of the White House.
after all,
I AM BLACK,
and buildings can't turn
seven times in a circle.

ARE WE WHAT WE EAT?

for Pedro Pietri

Physicians, dieticians, theologists, cult leaders,
gurus, and other authoritarians
have declared that we are indeed what we eat.
What we don't know is whether or not
this means that the things that enter our mouths
and end up in our stomachs are reflected
in our physical, mental, and spiritual well being
or do we become the thing itself.
If the latter is the case, would that mean
we function, behave, and think
like the things we put into our bodies?

Think about a man
who eats pork everyday of his life.
Can we expect this man to be pushy, greedy, filthy,
and lethal?
Then there's the man who can't live
without beef.
Should we assume that this man is on the offensive
everytime he sees red?
How about somebody who consumes a lot of turkey?
Chicken?
Do people on a strict seafood diet find themselves
consistently drawn to oceans, lakes, rivers, streams,
ponds, or puddles?
Is it safe to predict that a person who eats Twinkies
by the truckload will go mad, run amok,

and assassinate the assistant to the assistant janitor
down at city hall?
Vegetarians?
Do they stay in one place, continuously reach
for the sky and sway in whichever direction the wind
is blowing?
Imagine people in the habit of swallowing rocks.
Will that make them hard, cold, sedentary
and ill shaped?
Could it be said they get kicked and tossed around a lot?

If we are what we eat,
then what about what we drink?
Like to smell?
Smoke?
Believe?
Are all corn whiskey drinkers redneck crackers?
What do we say for the man who likes to sniff dirty
drawers
like some folks like to snort cocaine?
Should the man who free bases Drano
be considered a bit soft in the head?
Are all people who believe the government
has their best interests in mind hopeless psychotics
or backwards fantasizers?

If we are indeed what we put into our bodies,
then let us say bon appetit!

Meditation On A Get-Together For Ted At Jim's House

for Ted Pontiflet and Jim Lacy

I sit there,
watching you with them,
most of you old Mackites,
reminiscing,
dragging out the light
of ourstory,
then and now,
the mystery, myth, and real folk
that we be.
the spirit of these musics,
these portraits, these tales
we McClymonds grads—Warriors forever—
have carried and gifted
to freedom and fun loving people
everywhere.

when I am sixty,
let me gather together
in the good company and comraderie
of wise elders to drag out the light
of this time and place
when we macked down
West Oakland streets,
to sneak a peek
at the Temptations
or Smokey Robinson and the Miracles

at the old Continental Club on 12th and Peralta
like you all
tipped in at Slim Jenkin's
down on 7th to catch a riff or a chorus
when Duke, Count, or McShann
hit town.

when I reach the big six-O,
let me come together
with other Orishas of my time
to mash the light of our wisdom
on those to come,
keeping the nasty, hateful,
ugly, poisonous waste material
out of their reach.

1/12/94
12:30 am
Oakland

Reginald Lockett was born in Berkeley, California and grew up in West Oakland. He has taught literature, basic language skills, composition, critical thinking, and creative writing at San Francisco State University, Laney College, City College of San Francisco, and San Jose City College. His poetry, prose, reviews, short stories and articles have appeared in over fifty anthologies and periodicals. He presently performs with the WordWind Chorus and lives and writes in Oakland.